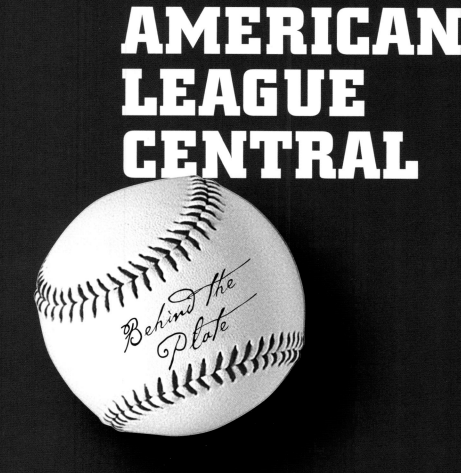

AMERICAN LEAGUE CENTRAL

Behind the Plate

By David Fischer

THE CHICAGO WHITE SOX, THE CLEVELAND INDIANS, THE DETROIT TIGERS, THE KANSAS CITY ROYALS, AND THE MINNESOTA TWINS

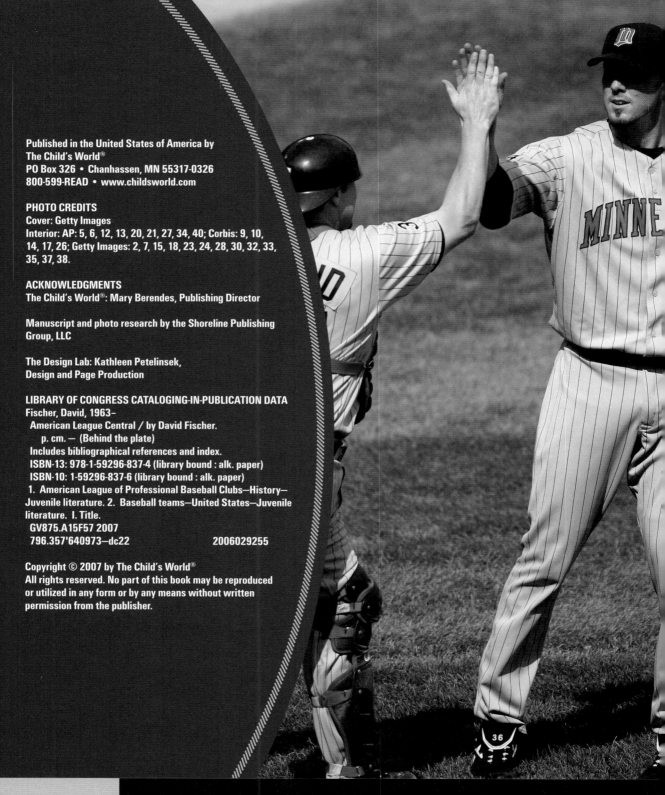

Published in the United States of America by
The Child's World®
PO Box 326 • Chanhassen, MN 55317-0326
800-599-READ • www.childsworld.com

PHOTO CREDITS
Cover: Getty Images
Interior: AP: 5, 6, 12, 13, 20, 21, 27, 34, 40; Corbis: 9, 10,
14, 17, 26; Getty Images: 2, 7, 15, 18, 23, 24, 28, 30, 32, 33,
35, 37, 38.

ACKNOWLEDGMENTS
The Child's World®: Mary Berendes, Publishing Director

Manuscript and photo research by the Shoreline Publishing
Group, LLC

The Design Lab: Kathleen Petelinsek,
Design and Page Production

LIBRARY OF CONGRESS CATALOGING-IN-PUBLICATION DATA
Fischer, David, 1963–
  American League Central / by David Fischer.
    p. cm. — (Behind the plate)
  Includes bibliographical references and index.
  ISBN-13: 978-1-59296-837-4 (library bound : alk. paper)
  ISBN-10: 1-59296-837-6 (library bound : alk. paper)
  1. American League of Professional Baseball Clubs—History—
Juvenile literature. 2. Baseball teams—United States—Juvenile
literature. I. Title.
  GV875.A15F57 2007
  796.357'640973—dc22   2006029255

The Twins won the AL Central in 2006. On the cover: Minnesota pitcher Johan Santana.

Contents

INTRODUCTION

The American League (AL) Central was baseball's best and most exciting division during the 2006 season. Oh, you might get a few arguments from fans of the AL East—where the New York Yankees and Boston Red Sox grabbed more headlines—or from fans of the NL West—where all five teams were in the title chase through most of the summer. But the AL Central featured three of the best teams in the majors in the Detroit Tigers, the Chicago White Sox, and the Minnesota Twins. They gave baseball fans quite a show all season.

Then again, those teams have been entertaining AL fans for a long time. All three clubs, in fact, were **charter members** of the league in 1901 (the Twins were located in Washington, D.C., at the time). Another current member of the AL Central, the Cleveland Indians, also was among the eight franchises that played in the AL in 1901. Only the Kansas City Royals, who began play in 1969, don't go so far back.

The Royals, however, do go back to the beginning of the AL Central in 1994. That year, Major League Baseball **realigned** into three divisions in

AMERICAN LEAGUE CENTRAL TEAMS:

Chicago White Sox
Founded: 1901
Park: U.S. Cellular Field
Park Opened: 1991
Colors: Black and gray

Cleveland Indians
Founded: 1901
Park: Jacobs Field
Park Opened: 1994
Colors: Navy blue and red

Detroit Tigers
Founded: 1901
Park: Comerica Park
Park Opened: 2000
Colors: Navy blue and orange

Kansas City Royals
Founded: 1969
Park: Kauffman Stadium
Park Opened: 1973
Color: Royal blue and white

Minnesota Twins
Founded: 1901
Park: Hubert H. Humphrey Metrodome
Park Opened: 1982
Colors: Navy blue and red

The Tigers and White Sox were two of the original members of the American League in 1901. They battled toe-to-toe in an exciting 2006 division title chase.

each league for the first time. Previously, the AL's 14 teams had been split into two divisions, with seven teams in the East and seven teams in the West. But in 1994, three former AL West teams—the White Sox, Royals, and Twins—were placed in the newly formed Central. Two former AL East teams—the Indians and the Milwaukee Brewers—joined them.

Five years later, the big leagues added two **expansion franchises**: Tampa Bay in the AL and Arizona in the NL. But that meant there were 15 teams in each league. In order to keep an even number of teams in each league (otherwise one team wouldn't be able to play every day), the Brewers left the AL Central to join the NL Central. Tampa Bay was placed in the AL East, and the Detroit Tigers shifted from the AL East to join the White Sox, Indians, Royals, and Twins in the Central. The division has stayed the same ever since.

That's a quick overview on how the AL Central came to be. Now, read on to learn more about each of the five franchises in this exciting division.

The Indians and Royals finished well behind the top three in the Central Division in 2006. But each of those clubs has had some storied seasons in its history.

THE CHICAGO WHITE SOX

When first base-man Paul Konerko squeezed Juan Uribe's throw from shortstop for the final out in Chicago's 1–0 victory over the Houston Astros in Game 4 of the 2005 World Series, the White Sox were the champions of baseball for the first time in 88 years. By winning, the White Sox capped a dream season in which they won 99 regular-season games, then added 11 victories in 12 tries in postseason games against the Boston Red Sox, Los Angeles Angels, and the Astros.

The city of Chicago took time out to celebrate the White Sox' World Series championship in 2005 with a ticker-tape parade.

CHAPTER ONE

The 2005 White Sox also helped erase the **stigma** of one of the darkest periods in baseball history. That came in 1919, two years after Chicago had last won the World Series with a six-game victory over the New York Giants. (The 1917 crown was the second title in their history; the first came in a six-game victory over the cross-town rival Cubs in the 1906 World Series.) The powerful White Sox, with stars such as pitcher Eddie Cicotte, outfielders Happy Felsch and "Shoeless" Joe Jackson, and infielders Eddie Collins and Buck Weaver, had rolled through their AL schedule in 1919, winning 88 games and losing just 52.

But White Sox owner Charles Comiskey, who had been an instrumental figure in form-ing the AL in 1901, was known for his penny-pinching ways. He underpaid his players. He didn't always have the uniforms washed to cut down on the laundry bill. And he reportedly gave the players a case of cheap champagne for winning the 1917 pennant instead of follow-ing through on a promise of giving them all a bonus (or maybe that's what he considered a bo-nus!). So the White Sox players were targets for gamblers, who approached them to "fix" the 1919

"Big Ed" Walsh was a workhorse pitcher for the White Sox in the early days of the franchise. In 1908, he won 40 games—the second most in the big leagues in post-1900 history—while pitching 464 innings. Twice in his career, he started and won both ends of a doubleheader.

Chicago Tribune sports editor Arch Ward proposed the idea of the first All-Star Game in 1933. That game, which was played at the White Sox's Comiskey Park, was such a big hit that it became an annual event.

Eddie Collins is one of the greatest players in White Sox history. The Hall of Famer played more games at second base than anyone else in baseball history.

World Series against the Reds—that is, to lose on purpose in exchange for money.

The heavily favored White Sox did indeed lose, five games to three. Several of Chicago's best players made uncharacteristic fielding errors, pitching mistakes, and base-running blunders. Such mistakes in no way resembled their quality of play during the regular season. Rumors spread that the White Sox had intentionally lost. Baseball fans were outraged, and the team became known as the Black Sox. Team owners and league officials were concerned. Even the slightest hint of gamblers' involvement would spoil baseball's honest image. The owners worried that fans would lose faith in the game's **integrity**. So they hired a federal judge named Kenesaw Mountain Landis to become baseball's first commissioner.

The formidable White Sox went 88-52 during the 1919 regular season. But the World Series scandal has forever left that team's legacy tainted.

Former White Sox outfielder Minnie Minoso is the only man to play in five different decades. Minoso got his start in 1949 with Cleveland before coming to Chicago in 1952. He retired, at least initially, in 1964. In 1976, as part publicity gimmick and part favor to his old friend, White Sox owner Bill Veeck signed Minoso to a short-term contract. He played in three games at age 53, getting one hit in eight at bats. Four years later, Minoso pinch-hit in two games at age 57 (he did not get a hit).

Tony LaRussa, who managed the St. Louis Cardinals to a World Series victory in 2006, got his start as the rookie 34-year-old skipper of the White Sox in 1979. In 1983, LaRussa guided a surprising Chicago team to 99 regular-season wins and its first postseason appearance in 24 years.

In 1920, it was revealed that seven players—including Jackson and Cicotte—had accepted bribes from gamblers to purposely lose the 1919 World Series. One player, Weaver, sat in on the secret meetings, even though he did not accept bribes. Though they were cleared in a court of law, it made no matter to Judge Landis. All eight players were banned from baseball for life.

For the next three decades, the White Sox struggled, only occasionally winning more games than they lost. Then, in 1951, with newly acquired Minnie Minoso batting .324, Chicago went 81–73 to begin a remarkable string of 17 consecutive winning seasons.

In 1958, the team got a new owner, Bill Veeck, the former top man of the Cleveland Indians and St. Louis Browns. Veeck was a showman who set attendance records at each stop. During an inventive career, he introduced a midget player (Eddie Gaedel), fireworks, Bat Day, exploding scoreboards, and player names on the backs of uniforms.

One year later, the White Sox won their first AL pennant in 40 years. Early Wynn won 22 games to lead the league's best pitching staff. The

offense, which led the majors in stolen bases, was jump-started by shortstop Luis Aparicio and second baseman Nellie Fox. On the night they clinched the pennant, White Sox fans felt as if a curse had been lifted. The "Go-Go Sox," as they were called, faced the Dodgers in the World Series, but lost.

In would be 24 years before the White Sox returned to the post-season. In 1983, Manager Tony LaRussa led them to their first AL West championship. The club also won division titles in 1993 and 2000, but failed each time to advance to the World Series. Frank Thomas, a hulking, 6-foot 5-inch, 257-pound first baseman, established himself as one

First baseman Frank Thomas was nicknamed "The Big Hurt." He put the hurt on opposing teams by mashing 448 home runs in 16 seasons for Chicago.

of the most intimidating batters in team history. "The Big Hurt" hit more than .300, scored more than 100 runs, drove in at least 100 runs, and walked more than 100 times every season from 1991 to 1997. He won two MVP awards.

In 2004, Konerko succeeded Thomas as the White Sox's biggest threat on offense. Konerko hit 35 or more home runs and drove in more than 100 runs three consecutive seasons through 2006. He had plenty of help, too, on the White Sox's championship team in 2005. Though none of the club's eight regular starters batted .300, seven of them reached double figures in home runs. The eighth, outfielder Scott Podsednik, finished second in the league with 59 stolen bases.

Paul Konerko is a powerful force on offense. He hit 35 homers and drove in 113 runs in 2006—his fourth season in five years with more than 100 RBIs.

14

THE CLEVELAND INDIANS

After failing to win a division title in 25 seasons in the AL East from 1969 to 1993, the Cleveland Indians welcomed the move to the new AL Central in 1994. The following year, they began a string of five consecutive division championships (and six crowns in a seven-year span). They reached the World Series twice in the 1990s, but are still in pursuit of their first championship since 1948.

Club president Bill Veeck (center) and shortstop and manager Lou Boudreau (in uniform) celebrated after the Indians won the 1948 World Series.

Cleveland, which originally was known as the Blues, was a charter member of the AL in 1901. Though they did not win a pennant until 1920, the franchise did feature one of the league's earliest stars in second baseman Nap Lajoie (pronounced la-ZHO-way), who was acquired from the Philadelphia Athletics in 1902. While with Cleveland, Lajoie won the AL batting crown in 1903 and 1904. Turnstiles at League Park spun as fans turned out to see Lajoie, whose sparkling play saved the franchise. In 1905, he became **player-manager** of the club.

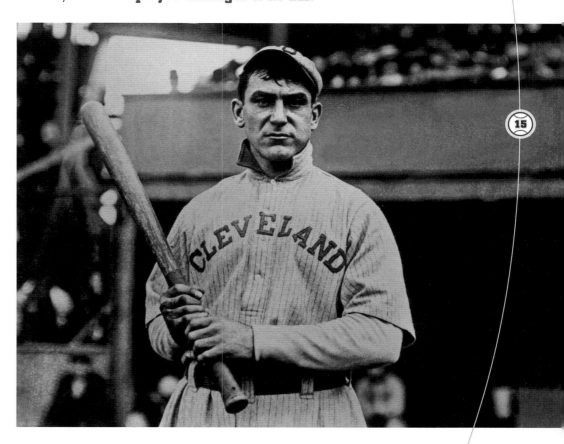

Nap Lajoie was so popular in Cleveland that, for a time, the franchise was named for him (the "Naps"). Later, he became the first second baseman to make the Hall of Fame.

16

After one season, the Blues' name was changed to the Broncos, but that wasn't popular. So a Cleveland newspaper held a contest to find a better name. The winning entry was the Naps, after Nap Lajoie. Fans so adored their graceful second baseman that the name lasted as long as he remained in Cleveland.

Lajoie was released in 1914, and another newspaper contest was held to rename the team. This time, the winning entry was Indians. Fans had suggested the name in honor of Louis "Chief" Sockalexis, the first Native American to play **professional** baseball. Sockalexis, who became a legend while playing for the NL's Cleveland Spiders before the turn of the century, had died in 1913 at age 42.

Tris Speaker joined the Indians in 1916 and became the club's next big star. A daring centerfielder, Speaker often played shallow, chasing down short flies and making plays in the infield. As a result, he threw out more base runners (449) and was part of more double plays (139) than any other outfielder in history.

While still a player, Speaker also took over as manager of the Indians in 1919. The following season, Cleveland won its first World Series, beating

Jim Bagby, Sr., led the American League when he won 31 games for the Indians' World Series champions in 1920. His son, Jim Jr., pitched for the Tribe in the 1940s and is remembered as the relief pitcher who helped snap Joe DiMaggio's record 56-game hitting streak in 1941.

The Indians' Bob Feller is the only pitcher to throw a no-hitter on Opening Day. It came in 1940, when the future Hall of Famer was just 21 years old. He blanked the White Sox 1–0 in a game in Chicago in which he struck out eight batters. Feller would go on to pitch three no-hitters in his career; he also had a remarkable 12 one-hitters, a record he shares with Nolan Ryan.

Center fielder Tris Speaker was a star on both offense and defense beginning in 1916. Eventually, he took over as manager and led the Indians to their first World Series win.

Brooklyn five games to two. The most memorable moment was second baseman Bill Wambsganss's unassisted triple play. With runners on first and second going on Clarence Mitchell's line drive, Wambsganss snared the ball for the first out, stepped on second to force another runner out, and tagged the runner coming from first for the third out!

The Indians did not return to the postseason until 1948. That year, long-time player Bob Feller—the greatest pitcher in Indians' history—led the AL in strikeouts for the seventh time. After winning the pennant, the team downed the Boston Braves in six games in the World Series. Cleveland hasn't won another title since.

The 1954 Indians had a stellar pitching staff that included three future Hall of Fame starters—Feller, Bob Lemon, and Early Wynn. Another Hall of Famer, Larry Doby, topped the league in homers and RBIs. The

Sandy Alomar was a key player for the Indians' 1997 pennant winners. Cleveland fans will always remember his homer against the Yankees in Game Four of the Division Series.

formidable team won a league-record 111 games out of 154. But the season ended on a sour note as the Indians lost the World Series to the New York Giants in four straight games.

Bad breaks and bad decisions soon doomed the Indians, and Cleveland suffered a postseason drought that lasted 41 years. Finally, playing in new Jacobs Field, the team began its run of Central Division titles in 1995. The Indians advanced to the World Series that season, then again in 1997, but both times were unable to win a long-awaited title. In 1995, paced by moody slugger Albert Belle's 50 home runs, the Indians won 100 games and ran away with the division by 30 games, the largest margin ever. Despite falling to Atlanta in the World Series, Cleveland loved the Indians. The fans bought every available ticket for 455 straight games—a major-league record for most consecutive sellouts.

The Indians' dash to the World Series in 1997 was thrilling. Facing elimination in Game 4 of the American League Division Series (ALDS) against the Yankees, Sandy Alomar's dramatic home run in the eighth inning tied the game, and the Indians rallied to win the series. Then the Indians

beat the Orioles in Game 6 of the AL Championship Series (ALCS) on an 11th-inning home run by Tony Fernandez. The World Series went seven games and was decided in extra innings, but the Florida Marlins were the winners.

Jim Thome, Kenny Lofton, and Roberto Alomar led a potent offense that carried the Indians to another division crown in 2001. But after a disappointing first-round playoff loss, all the stars of the 1990s eventually were let go. New stars have filled their place. Designated hitter Travis Hafner batted .305 with 33 home runs and 108 runs batted in (RBIs) for the Indians in 2005. The team went 93–69 and narrowly missed a wild-card playoff berth. Young pitcher Cliff Lee won 18 games that season. But the Indians failed to build on their '05 performance and slumped near the bottom of the standings in 2006.

The Indians may have slumped in 2006, but designated hitter Travis Hafner didn't. He batted .308 with 42 home runs and 117 runs batted in that year.

21

THE DETROIT TIGERS

After more than a decade of poor play, the Detroit Tigers were the major leagues' feel-good story of the year in 2006. Detroit entered the season having posted a losing record in 12 consecutive years, including a disastrous 43–119 mark in 2003 that marked the low point in club history. After a 71–91 season in 2005, the club replaced popular former infielder Alan Trammell with veteran Jim Leyland as manager.

The Tigers greeted Magglio Ordonez (30) after his ninth-inning home run beat the A's in the 2006 playoffs and sent Detroit to the World Series for the first time in 22 years.

CHAPTER THREE

Though Leyland had guided the fifth-year Florida Marlins to a World Series victory in 1997, he had not managed in the big leagues since 1999, and little was expected of Detroit. Even after the Tigers roared to five consecutive victories to start the season, most baseball experts figured the club would come back to earth. Detroit never let up, however. By the All-Star Break, the Tigers sported a big-league-best 59–29 record. Detroit went on to finish 95–67 and earn a trip to the postseason as a **wild-card team**.

The return to the playoffs was welcome news for Tigers' fans who had been accustomed to success almost from the beginning of Detroit's history. The Tigers went 74–61 to finish a respectable third in their first season in the new AL in 1901. By 1907, the club began a string of three consecutive league pennants under Manager Hughie Jennings. Not coincidentally, that also was the first year that 20-year-old Ty Cobb became a regular for the Tigers. Baseball's biggest star before Babe Ruth, and one of the greatest players in major-league history, Cobb's career batting average of .367 is the highest ever. He won 12 batting titles and was the first player to amass 4,000 hits for his career. A ferocious

In the first game in their history in 1901, the Tigers entered the bottom of the ninth inning trailing the Milwaukee Brewers 13–4. Remarkably, they proceeded to score 10 runs—the last two came on Frank Dillon's game-winning double—to thrill the home crowd at Bennett Park with a 14–13 win.

In 1905, the Tigers acquired Ty Cobb from Augusta in the Sally League in exchange for 21-year-old pitcher Eddie Cicotte and cash. Cobb, of course, went on to a Hall of Fame career. Cicotte would win 208 big-league games in his career, but became notorious as one of the players involved in the "Chicago Black Sox" scandal of 1919.

Ty Cobb was one of baseball's all-time greats. After batting .366 and stealing 892 bases in 24 big-league seasons, he was one of the inaugural members of the Hall of Fame.

competitor and a tenacious base runner, Cobb's 892 career stolen bases stood as a record for 50 years.

Despite Cobb's play, the Tigers failed to win a World Series during his tenure. Detroit's next pennant came in 1934, when four future Hall of Famers—catcher-manager Mickey Cochrane, first baseman Hank Greenberg, outfielder Goose Goslin, and second baseman Charlie Gehringer—helped the team win 101 regular-season games. Again, though, the Tigers lost in the World Series.

Slugging first baseman Hank Greenberg made his debut with the Tigers at age 19 in 1930. He was one of several future Hall of Famers who helped Detroit win the pennant in 1934.

Detroit returned to the Series the next year and was determined to succeed. Cochrane's daring dash from second base on Goslin's clutch single in the bottom of the ninth inning of Game Six scored the Series-winning run. The Tigers were champions at last.

In 1940, pitcher Bobo Newsom won 21 games, and the Tigers won their sixth pennant. Newsom won two more games in the World Series against Cincinnati and was working on one day's rest in the deciding Game Seven. If ever there was a sentimental favorite, it was Bobo, whose father had died a day after watching his son win Game One. Bobo dedicated his Game Five shutout to his dad, but then was a tough-luck loser in the finale, 2–1.

Many baseball players had left the game by 1945 to serve in the military during World War II. Greenberg returned from his army service in midseason and worked his way into shape as Detroit and Washington tied for first place. On the season's final day, Greenberg hit a dramatic, come-from-behind grand slam (a home run with the bases loaded) in the ninth inning to clinch the pennant for Detroit. Then the Tigers knocked off the Cubs in seven games and won their second World Series title.

The Tigers didn't win another pennant for 23 years and came close only twice. Talented new players such as George Kell and Al Kaline each won a batting title. Kaline won his in 1955—with a .340 average—at age 20, making him the youngest player in history to earn a batting title.

The Tigers snapped their championship drought behind Denny McLain's 31–6 record on the mound in 1968. (No pitcher has won 30 or more games in a season since.) McLain wasn't as effective in the World Series against the St. Louis Cardinals, but Mickey Lolich made up for it. He won three games, including Game Seven, and the Tigers won their third title.

In 1984, under Manager Sparky Anderson, the Tigers were head and shoulders above the rest of the AL. They remained in first place from the first game to the last. Led by outfielder Kirk Gibson and middle

Kirk Gibson and the 1984 Tigers got off to the fastest start (35-5) in big-league history. By season's end, they were World Series champions.

infielders Trammell and Lou Whitaker, Detroit vaulted into first place by winning its first nine games. The Tigers ended April at 18–2, and were 35–5 in late May—the best 40-game start in major-league history. The Tigers finished with a 104–58 record, 15 games in front of the pack. They swept aside the Kansas City Royals in the AL playoffs, then beat the San Diego Padres to win their fourth World Series.

After another division title in 1987, though, defeat became routine. But in 2004, former All-Star catcher Ivan Rodriguez signed with the Tigers as a **free agent**. A fierce competitor, he helped change the losing climate. One year later, another former All-Star, outfielder Magglio Ordonez, signed. Those two proved to be key cogs in the club's thrilling 2006 season, during which the Tigers won their first AL pennant in 22 years before falling to the Cardinals in five games in the World Series.

All-Star catcher Ivan Rodriguez was a key free-agent addition for the Tigers in 2004 and soon helped point the way to the World Series.

Kauffman Stadium
12:59   1 2 3 4 5 6 7 8 9   R H E
JAYS   0 0 0
ROYALS   0 0 0
BALL   STRIKE   OUT
  0   0   0
         AT BAT
           37
10   5   20
HOWSER   BRETT   WHITE

THE KANSAS CITY ROYALS

Perhaps no other team in baseball currently epitomizes the struggle between the big-market clubs and the small-market teams than the Kansas City Royals. The economics of baseball are such that big-market franchises (such as the New York Yankees) can generate more revenue from resources like television contracts and advertising and thus can afford to pay their current players more and attract better talent through free agency. Smaller-market teams (such as the Royals) can't always afford to hold on to the good young players they develop because those players eventually go elsewhere to earn more money.

CHAPTER FOUR   Kauffman Stadium has been the Royals' home since 1973. In recent years, the Royals have struggled to keep pace with the bigger-market franchises.

Despite annually facing such a **dilemma**, however, the Royals have seven postseason appearances and one World Series win in their relatively brief history. All of those playoff seasons came in a 10-year span from 1976 to 1985 in which the Royals boasted some of the majors' best teams.

The Royals began as an expansion team in 1969. Only two years earlier, the Kansas City Athletics had left town and moved to Oakland. The new club was placed in the AL West and played its games at Municipal Stadium until 1973, when the team moved into Royals Stadium (now called Kauffman Stadium). The beautiful new stadium featured water fountains beyond the outfield fence and an electronic scoreboard that stood 10 stories high. Since the infield and outfield at Royals Stadium were carpeted with an artificial surface and the outfield fences were very deep, management set out to build a team around speed, pitching, and defense. That proved to be a wise decision.

After several second-place finishes, Manager Whitey Herzog's team won the AL West for the first time in 1976. Third baseman George Brett led the league with 215 hits and a .333 average, winning

his first batting crown by one point over teammate Hal McRae. Brett hit .300 or better 11 times during his career. He was the heart and soul of a Royals' team that won three consecutive division titles.

All three times, though, the Royals failed to reach the World Series because they could not beat the New York Yankees. Twice, the Royals battled the Yankees to the limit, only to have the pennant snatched away in the final inning of the final game of the ALCS.

The Royals had a sizzling season in 1980 under new manager Jim Frey and won the division for the fourth time in five years. Brett was the AL MVP with a .390 batting average, the highest mark since legendary Red Sox star Ted Williams hit .406 in 1941. Right-handed pitcher Dennis Leonard was a 20-game winner for the third time in four seasons. Speedy outfielder Willie Wilson led the league with 230 hits.

Best of all, on their fourth try, Kansas City finally **vanquished** the Yankees in a three-game sweep to capture the pennant. Brett blasted a dramatic home run off Rich "Goose" Gossage at Yankee Stadium to propel the Royals to their first World Series. But despite the best efforts of first baseman Willie Aikens (who batted .400 with four

George Brett was an incredibly gifted batter who amassed 3,154 hits in his 21-season big-league career—all of it with the Royals. In 1999, he was inducted into the Hall of Fame.

homers) and centerfielder Amos Otis (who hit .478 with three homers), the team lost to the Philadelphia Phillies in six games.

The Royals finally reached the top of the baseball world under Manager Dick Howser in 1985. Bret Saberhagen, a 21-year-old pitcher, was a surprising 20-game winner. He earned the **Cy Young Award** in just his second season. Dan Quisenberry, a tall, paper-thin relief pitcher, led the league in **saves** for the fourth straight year. The Royals rallied from a three-games-to-one deficit to the Toronto Blue Jays in the ALCS to win their second pennant.

To win the World Series against the cross-state rival St. Louis Cardinals, the Royals needed another amazing comeback. Again, the team was down three games to one and on the brink of elimination. But

Reliever Dan Quisenberry had a unique delivery that submarined many opposing batters. Quisenberry led the AL in saves each year from 1982 to 1985.

the Royals won Game Five in St. Louis to send the Series back to Kansas City. With the team trailing by one run in the bottom of the ninth inning of Game Six, Royals pinch hitter Jorge Orta was ruled safe on a controversial call at first base. Television replays showed that he was clearly out. The umpire's bad call opened the door to a dramatic rally, capped by Dane Iorg's single that sent home the tying and winning runs.

In the seventh and deciding game, Saberhagen was pitching the most pressure-packed game of his life, yet he wasn't a bit nervous. During the game, he flashed messages from the bench to his pregnant

Bret Saberhagen was just 21 years old when he won 20 regular-season games in 1985. He was unfazed by postseason pressure, too, and won Game Seven of the World Series.

wife, who was due to deliver their child at any moment. The sopho-more sensation tossed a complete-game shutout, and the Royals had accomplished the improbable mission of winning three games in a row in back-to-back series.

Since then, the Royals have not been back to the playoffs. Frustrated fans complain that the ability of big-market teams to spend lavishly on players hurts Kansas City's chances of competing. They point to superstars such as Johnny Damon, Jermaine Dye, and Carlos Beltran. All of them had to be traded away because they were about to become free agents.

Still, a Royals' team of overachievers remained in pennant conten-tion through most of the summer in 2003. Several poor seasons have followed. One bright spot in an otherwise dismal 2006 season was the development of young third baseman Mark Teahen, who came up from the minors for good in June and batted .290 with 18 home runs.

Third baseman Mark Teahen is an emerging star for the Royals. Though he played in only 109 games in the Majors in 2006, he batted .290 and hit 18 home runs.

35

THE MINNESOTA TWINS

In the early 2000s, as Major League Baseball struggled to find a solution to the disparity between big-market and small-market teams, the Minnesota Twins were on the verge of being dissolved. One of the smaller-market franchises, the Twins couldn't pay their players as much as the big-market teams could. Their attendance ranked near the bottom of the American League. On the field, they had little success since last winning the World Series in 1991.

The Twins thrilled the home fans by winning all four games at the Metrodome in a seven-game World Series triumph over the Atlanta Braves in 1991.

Now those days seem so long ago! Because not only did the Twins survive, but they have thrived since then. In 2002, the very year it was reported that they soon would no longer exist, the Twins began a string of three consecutive 90-win seasons and three consecutive AL Central Division championships.

The Twins' rapid rise back to the top in the decade of the 2000s should come as no surprise to followers of the club, however. That's because being a Twins' fan is like sitting on a seesaw. You experience a lot of ups and downs. That includes the wildest ride in big-league history: In 1991, the Twins became the first big-league team to catapult from a last-place finish to World Series champion in only one year.

The Twins have played in Minnesota since 1961, but the roots of the franchise go back to 1901. That year, the franchise began play as the Senators, an original member of the AL based in Washington, D.C. The Senators had a few good years, even winning the World Series in 1924, but more often than not, they resided in the bottom half of the league standings each year.

In 1961, the franchise moved to the Twin Cities area of Minneapolis and St. Paul in Minnesota—

Cesar Tovar was a versatile player for the Twins from 1965 to 1972. How versatile was he? Well, in one game late in the 1968 season, he played all nine defensive positions. He started the game at pitcher, tossing one scoreless inning against the A's in a game the Twins went on to win, 2–1.

The Twins are the only team ever to turn two triple plays in one game. It happened at Boston on July 17, 1990, and both triple plays were started by third baseman Gary Gaetti. Believe it or not, though, Minnesota lost the game 1–0. The Red Sox's lone run was unearned and scored the result of—you guessed it—an error by Gaetti!

Harmon Killebrew brought his big bat from Washington to Minnesota when the franchise moved to the Twin Cities in 1961. He belted 573 homers in his 22 big-league seasons.

38

hence, the name Minnesota Twins. The Twins' first star was slugger Harmon Killebrew, a holdover from the club's days in Washington. Killebrew hit 45 or more home runs in each of the Twins first four seasons in Minnesota.

Killebrew and outfielder Tony Oliva formed a potent one-two punch. Oliva got on base, and Killebrew knocked him home. Manager Sam Mele's club was an offensive powerhouse that breezed to the AL pennant in 1965 without much of a challenge. The Twins' big hitters

Kirby Puckett (left) and Kent Hrbek starred together on the Twins' 1991 champs. Puckett batted .319 that season while Hrbek slugged 20 home runs.

couldn't overcome the Dodgers' pitching in the World Series, though. Los Angeles **ace** Sandy Koufax shattered the Twins' bats—and their hopes—with a three-hit shutout in the deciding Game 7 at Minnesota's Metropolitan Stadium.

Two years later, a young infielder from Panama named Rod Carew made his debut for the Twins. A left-handed hitter with an effortless swing and uncanny bat control, Carew had the ability to redirect a pitched ball safely between infielders or in front of outfielders. Using a variety of batting stances, Carew was the league's leading hitter seven times in his 12 seasons with the Twins. Carew's first batting crown came in 1969, when he hit .332 to help the Twins win the first of back-to-back AL West titles. Minnesota fell to Baltimore in the ALCS both times, though.

After that, it wasn't until the mid-1980s that the Twins would again be a serious contender. Centerfielder Kirby Puckett and first baseman Kent Hrbek developed their talents under the steady hand of Manager Tom Kelly. New owner Carl Pohlad allowed time for the prospects to hone their skills in a new indoor stadium called the Metrodome. The Metrodome would prove to give the Twins a huge

home-field advantage. In 1987, the Twins reached the World Series for the first time in 22 years. The Series against the St. Louis Cardinals was played indoors for the first time. Minnesota fans enthusiastically waved "Homer Hankies" and cheered so loudly that the noise level inside the dome was equal to the sound of a jet engine. Inspired by the excitement, the Twins won all four games played in the "Homer Dome" and won the World Series in seven games.

By 1990, the Twins were again a last-place team. But, in perhaps the most unbelievable turnaround in baseball history, the Twins cata-

First baseman Justin Morneau had a monster season for the Twins in 2006. He batted .321 with 34 home runs, and was named the AL's Most Valuable Player.

pulted over the rest of the West Division and then beat the Toronto Blue Jays in the playoffs.

The 1991 World Series against the Atlanta Braves was a gut-wrenching test of nerves. Minnesota won the first two games, while Atlanta won the next three and needed just one more victory to capture the title. But the Twins were playing in the Dome, and their beloved hometown hero, Kirby Puckett, refused to let his team lose. He made a spectacular leaping catch at the centerfield wall in extra innings to save the game. Then, leading off the bottom of the 11th, Puckett smashed a home run to give the Twins a dramatic victory. The next night, after a 1–0 win in 10 innings in Game Seven, the Twins were world champions for the second time in five years.

The rest of the 1990s were not as successful, and in 1999 the Twins had the AL's worst record. But by 2002, they were led by new manager Ron Gardenhire's never-say-die attitude and the flashy brilliance of cen-terfielder Torii Hunter. With their help, and with the emergence of Johan Santana as one of baseball's best starting pitchers, the Twins fashioned their three consecutive AL Central titles. Then, after a third-place finish in 2005, the club got off to a slow start in 2006. But with youngsters such as Joe Mauer, Justin Morneau, and Michael Cuddyer blossoming into stars, the Twins suddenly caught fire. A lengthy mid-season stretch of 34 victories in 42 games was the best in club history and propelled the Twins into the thick of the division chase. A victory over the White Sox on the last day of the season pushed the Twins past the Tigers by one game to win the Central. Not even a three-game sweep by the A's in the Division Series could spoil a memorable season.

STAT STUFF

TEAM RECORDS (THROUGH 2006)

Team	All-time Record	World Series Titles (Most Recent)	Number of Times in the Postseason	Top Manager (Wins)
Chicago	8,300–8,092	3 (2005)	8	Jimmie Dykes (899)
Cleveland	8,380–8,030	2 (1948)	9	Lou Boudreau (728)
Detroit	8,316–8,117	4 (1984)	12	Sparky Anderson (1,331)
Kansas City	2,934–3,083	1 (1985)	7	Whitey Herzog (410)
Minnesota*	7,884–8,514	3 (1991)	12	Bucky Harris (1,336)

*includes Washington

AMERICAN LEAGUE CENTRAL CAREER LEADERS (THROUGH 2006)

CHICAGO

Category	Name (Years with Team)	Total
Batting Average	Joe Jackson (1915–1920)	.340
Home Runs	Frank Thomas (1990–2005)	448
RBI	Frank Thomas (1990–2005)	1,465
Stolen Bases	Eddie Collins (1915–1926)	368
Wins	Ted Lyons (1923–1942, 1946)	260
Saves	Bobby Thigpen (1986–1993)	201
Strikeouts	Billy Pierce (1949–1961)	1,796

AMERICAN LEAGUE CENTRAL CAREER LEADERS (THROUGH 2006)

CLEVELAND

Category	Name (Years with Team)	Total
Batting Average	Joe Jackson (1910–1915)	.375
Home Runs	Jim Thome (1991–2002)	334
RBI	Earl Averill (1929–1939)	1,084
Stolen Bases	Kenny Lofton (1992–96, 1998–2001)	450
Wins	Bob Feller (1936–1941, 1945–1956)	266
Saves	Bob Wickman (2000–06)	139
Strikeouts	Bob Feller (1936–1941, 1945–1956)	2,581

DETROIT

Category	Name (Years with Team)	Total
Batting Average	Ty Cobb (1905–1926)	.369
Home Runs	Al Kaline (1953–1974)	399
RBI	Ty Cobb (1905–1926)	1,805
Stolen Bases	Ty Cobb (1905–1926)	865
Wins	Hooks Dauss (1912–1926)	223
Saves	Todd Jones (1997–2001, 2006)	179
Strikeouts	Mickey Lolich (1963–1975)	2,679

MORE STAT STUFF

AMERICAN LEAGUE CENTRAL CAREER LEADERS (THROUGH 2006)

KANSAS CITY

Category	Name (Years with Team)	Total
Batting Average	Jose Offerman (1996–98)	.306
Home Runs	George Brett (1973–1993)	317
RBI	George Brett (1973–1993)	1,595
Stolen Bases	Willie Wilson (1976–1990)	612
Wins	Paul Splittorff (1970–1984)	166
Saves	Jeff Montgomery (1988–1999)	304
Strikeouts	Kevin Appier (1989–1999, 2003–04)	1,458

MINNESOTA

Category	Name (Years with Team)	Total
Batting Average	Rod Carew (1967–1978)	.334
Home Runs	Harmon Killebrew (1954–1974)	559
RBI	Harmon Killebrew (1954–1974)	1,540
Stolen Bases	Clyde Milan (1907–1922)	495
Wins	Walter Johnson (1907–1927)	417
Saves	Rick Aguilera (1989–1999)	254
Strikeouts	Walter Johnson (1907–1927)	3,508

GLOSSARY

ace—the best starting pitcher on a team

charter members—original members of an organization

Cy Young Award—the award given each year to the best pitcher in the league (there are separate Cy Young Awards for the American and National Leagues)

dilemma—a serious problem

expansion franchises—new teams that start from scratch, thus increasing (or expanding) the total number of clubs in a given league

free agent—a player who has fulfilled his contract with one team and is free to sign with any other team

integrity—honesty; uprightness

player-manager—someone who takes over as a team's manager while remaining on the active roster; though rare today, it used to be a more common practice

professional— receiving pay for services or activities; in this case, playing baseball as a livelihood

realigned—organized its teams in a different way

saves—a statistical measure for a relief pitcher; he is credited with a save if he is the finishing pitcher, but not the winning pitcher, in a game his team won and he met one of the following criteria: he entered the game with the potential tying run either on base, at bat, or on deck; he pitched one complete inning and protected a lead of no more than three runs; or he pitched three innings.

stigma—something that detracts from a person's (or group's) reputation or character

vanquished—conquered; defeated

wild-card team—a team that finishes in second place in its division but still makes the playoffs by virtue of having the best record among a league's non-division winners

TIMELINE

1901 The AL is formed: The Chicago White Sox, Cleveland Indians, Detroit Tigers, and Washington Senators are among the charter members.

1907 Detroit wins the first of three consecutive AL pennants.

1917 The White Sox win the World Series for the second time in their relatively brief history.

1919 Baseball is rocked by the Chicago "Black Sox" scandal.

1920 The Indians win their first World Series.

1935 The Tigers win the World Series for the first time.

1954 Cleveland wins an AL-record 111 of 154 regular-season games, but is upset by the Giants in the World Series.

1961 The Washington Senators relocate to Minnesota and become the Twins.

1969 The Kansas City Royals begin play.

1985 The Royals win their first—and only—World Series.

1987 The Twins win the World Series; it's the second championship for the franchise, but the first since moving to Minnesota.

1991 Minnesota beats Atlanta in one of the most exciting World Series ever played.

2005 The White Sox roll to 99 regular-season victories, then win their first World Series in 88 years.

2006 Just three years removed from 119-loss season, the Tigers win their first AL pennant since 1984.

FOR MORE INFORMATION

BOOKS

Frisch, Aaron. *The History of the Minnesota Twins*. Mankato, Minn.: Creative Education, 2003.

Grabowski, John F. *The Chicago White Sox*. San Diego: Lucent Books, 2003.

Pietrusza, David, Matthew Silverman, and Michael Gershman (editors). *Baseball: The Biographical Encyclopedia*. New York: Total Sports, 2000.

Rambeck, Richard. *The Kansas City Royals: AL West*. Mankato, Minn.: Creative Education, 1992.

Schneider, Russell. *The Cleveland Indians Encyclopedia*. Philadelphia: Temple University Press, 1996.

Stewart, Wayne. *The History of the Detroit Tigers*. Mankato, Minn.: Creative Education, 2003.

ON THE WEB

Visit our home page for lots of links about the American League Central teams: ***http://www.childsworld.com/links***
Note to Parents, Teachers, and Librarians: We routinely check our Web links to make sure they're safe, active sites—so encourage your readers to check them out!

INDEX

ABOUT THE AUTHOR

David Fischer, a New Jersey-based author, has written several sports books, including *The Story of the New York Yankees, The Encyclopedia of the Summer Olympics,* **and** *The 50 Coolest Jobs in Sports.* **He has been published in** *Sports Illustrated for Kids,* **the** *New York Times,* **and** *Yankees Magazine,* **and has worked for** *Sports Illustrated,* **NBC Sports, and the** *National Sports Daily.*